THE SOURCES
OF A SCIENCE OF
EDUCATION

With this volume Kappa Delta Pi, an International Honor Society in Education, begins the publication of its series of lectures delivered annually at the Society's dinner by eminent scholars interested in the broad phases of education. Each lecture will be published as early as possible. Eventually the series will comprehend discussions by well known philosophers, scientists, educators and litterateurs whose combined interpretations of modern education should prove invaluable to professional and lay reader, alike.

THE SOURCES
OF A SCIENCE OF
EDUCATION

by
JOHN DEWEY

LIVERIGHT

NEW YORK

Originally published in 1929 by Horace Liveright

1.987654321

Standard Book Number: 87140-039-1
Library of Congress Catalog Card Number: 74-131280
MANUFACTURED IN THE UNITED STATES OF AMERICA

THE SOURCES
OF A SCIENCE OF
EDUCATION

The Sources of a Science of Education

[I]

EDUCATION AS A SCIENCE

THE title may suggest to some minds that it begs a prior question: *Is* there a science of education? And still more fundamentally, Can there be a science of education? Are the procedures and aims of education such that it is possible to reduce them to anything properly called a science? Similar questions exist in other fields. The issue is not unknown in history; it is raised in medicine and law. As far as education is concerned, I may confess at once that I have put the question in its apparently question-begging form in order to avoid discussion of questions that are important but that are also full of thorns and attended with controversial divisions.

It is enough for our purposes to note that the word "science" has a wide range.

There are those who would restrict the term to mathematics or to disciplines in which exact results can be determined by rigorous methods of demonstration. Such a conception limits even the claims of physics and chemistry to be sciences, for according to it the only scientific portion of these subjects is the strictly mathematical. The position of what are ordinarily termed the biological sciences is even more dubious, while social subjects and psychology would hardly rank as sciences at all, when measured by this definition. Clearly we must take the idea of science with some latitude. We must take it with sufficient looseness to include all the subjects that are usually regarded as sciences. The important thing is to discover those traits in virtue of which various fields are called scientific. When we raise the question in this way, we are led to put emphasis upon *methods* of dealing with subject-matter rather than to look for uniform objective traits in subject-matter. From this point of view, science signifies, I take it, the existence of systematic methods of inquiry, which, when they are brought to bear on a range of facts, enable us to understand them better and to control them more intelligently, less haphazardly and with less routine.

No one would doubt that our practices in hygiene and medicine are less casual, less results of a mixture of guess work and tradition, than they used to be, nor that this difference has been made by development of methods of investigating and testing. There is an intellectual technique by which discovery and organization of material go on cumulatively, and by means of which one inquirer can repeat the researches of another, confirm or discredit them, and add still more to the capital stock of knowledge. Moreover, the methods when they are used tend to perfect themselves, to suggest new problems, new investigations, which refine old procedures and create new and better ones.

The question as to the sources of a science of education is, then, to be taken in this sense. What are the ways by means of which the function of education in all its branches and phases —selection of material for the curriculum, methods of instruction and discipline, organization and administration of schools—can be conducted with systematic increase of intelligent control and understanding? What are the materials upon which we may—and should —draw in order that educational activities may become in a less degree products of routine, tradition, accident and transitory accidental influences? From what sources shall we draw so that there shall be steady and cumulative growth of intelligent, communicable insight and power of direction?

Here is the answer to those who decry pedagogical study on the ground that success in teaching and in moral direction of pupils is often not in any direct ratio to knowledge of educational principles. Here is "A" who is much more successful than "B" in teaching, awakening the enthusiasm of his students for learning, inspiring them morally by personal example and contact, and yet relatively ignorant of educational history, psychology, approved methods, etc., which "B" possesses in abundant measure. The facts are admitted. But what is overlooked by the objector is that the successes of such individuals tend to be born and to die with them: beneficial consequences extend only to those pupils who have personal contact with such gifted teachers. No one can measure the waste and loss that have come from the fact that the contributions of such men and women in the past have been thus confined, and the only way by which we can prevent such waste in the future is by methods which enable us to make an *analysis* of what the gifted teacher does intuitively, so that something accruing from his work can be communicated to others. Even in the things conventionally recorganized as sciences, the insights of unusual persons remain important and there is no levelling down to a uniform procedure. But the existence of science gives common efficacy to the experiences of the genius; it makes it possible for the results of special power to become part of the working equipment of other inquirers, instead of perishing as they arose.

The individual capacities of the Newtons, Boyles, Joules, Darwins, Lyells, Helmholtzes, are not destroyed because of the existence of science; their differences from others and the impossibility of predicting on the basis of past science what discoveries they would make— that is, the impossibility of regulating their activities by antecedent sciences—persist. But science makes it possible for others to benefit systematically by what they achieved.

The existence of scientific method protects us also from a danger that attends the operations of men of unusual power; dangers of slavish imitation partisanship, and such jealous devotion to them and their work as to get in the way of further progress. Anybody can notice to-day that the effect of an original and powerful teacher is not all to the good. Those influenced by him often show a one-sided interest; they tend to form schools, and to become impervious to other problems and truths; they incline to swear by the words of their master and to go on repeating his thoughts after him, and often without the spirit and insight that originally made them significant. Observation also shows that these results happen oftenest in those subjects in which scientific method is least developed. Where these methods are of longer standing students adopt methods rather than merely results, and employ them with flexibility rather than in literal reproduction.

This digression seems to be justified not merely because those who object to the idea of a science put personality and its unique gifts in opposition to science, but also because those who recommend science sometimes urge that uniformity of procedure will be its consequence. So it seems worth while to dwell on the fact that in the subjects best developed from the scientific point of view, the opposite is the case. Command of scientific methods and systematized subject-matter liberates individuals; it enables them to see new problems, devise new procedures, and, in general, makes for diversification rather than for set uniformity. But at the same time these diversifications have a cumulative effect in an advance shared by all workers in the field.

EDUCATION AS AN ART

THIS theme is, I think, closely connected with another point which is often urged, namely, that education is an art rather than a science. That, in concrete operation, education is an art, either a mechanical art or a fine art, is unquestionable. If there were an opposition between science and art, I should be compelled to side with those who assert that education is an art. But there is no opposition, although there is a distinction. We must not be misled by words. Engineering is, in actual practice, an art. But it is an art that progressively incorporates more and more of science into itself, more of mathematics, physics and chemistry. It is the kind of art it is precisely because of a content of scientific subject-matter which guides it as a practical operation. There is room for the original and daring projects of exceptional individuals. But their distinction lies not in the fact that they turn their backs upon science, but in the fact that they make new integrations of scientific material and turn it to new and previously unfamiliar and unforeseen uses. When, in education, the psychologist or observer and experimentalist in any field reduces his findings to a rule which is to be uniformly adopted, then, only, is there a result which is objectionable and destructive of the free play of education as an art.

But this happens not because of scientific method but because of departure from it. It is not the capable engineer who treats scientific findings as imposing upon him a certain course which is to be rigidly adhered to: it is the third- or fourth-rate man who adopts this course. Even more, it is the unskilled day laborer who follows it. For even if the practice adopted is one that follows from science and could not have been discovered or employed except for science, when it is converted into a uniform rule of procedure it becomes an empirical rule-of-thumb procedure—just as a person may use a table of logarithms mechanically without knowing anything about mathematics.

The danger is great in the degree in which the attempt to develop scientific method is recent. Nobody would deny that education is still in a condition of transition from an empirical to a scientific status. In its empirical form the chief factors determining education are tradition, imitative reproduction, response to various external pressures wherein the strongest force wins out, and the gifts, native and acquired, of individual teachers. In this situation there is a strong tendency to identify teaching ability with the use of procedures that yield immediately successful results, success being measured by such things as order in the classroom, correct recitations by pupils in assigned lessons, passing of examinations, promotion of pupils to a higher grade, etc.

For the most part, these are the standards by which a community judges the worth of a teacher. Prospective teachers come to training schools, whether in normal schools or colleges, with such ideas implicit in their minds. They want very largely to find out *how to do* things with the maximum prospect of success. Put baldly, they want recipes. Now, to such persons science is of value because it puts a stamp of final approval upon this and that specific procedure. It is very easy for science to be regarded as a guarantee that goes with the sale of goods rather than as a light to the eyes and a lamp to the feet. It is prized for its prestige value rather than as an organ of personal illumination and liberation. It is prized because it is thought to give unquestionable authenticity and authority to a specific procedure to be carried out in the school room. So conceived, science *is* antagonistic to education as an art.

––––––––––

Experience and Abstraction

The history of the more mature sciences shows two characteristics. Their original problems were set by difficulties that offered themselves in the ordinary region of practical affairs. Men obtained fire by rubbing sticks together and noted how things grew warm when they pressed on each other, long before they had any theory of heat. Such everyday experiences in their seeming inconsistency with the phenomena of flame and fire finally led to the conception of heat as a mode of molecular motion. But it led to this conception only when the ordinary phenomena were reflected upon in detachment from the conditions and uses under which they exhibit themselves in practices. There is no science without abstraction, and abstraction means fundamentally that certain occurrences are removed from the dimension of familiar practical experience into that of reflective or theoretical inquiry.

To be able to get away for the time being from entanglement in the urgencies and needs of immediate practical concerns is a condition of the origin of scientific treatment in any field. Preoccupation with attaining some direct end or practical utility, always limits scientific inquiry. For it restricts the field of attention and thought, since we note only those things that are immediately connected with what we want to do or get at the moment. Science signifies that we carry our observations and thinking further afield and become interested in what happens on its own account. Theory is in the end, as has been well said, the most practical of all things, because this widening of the range of attention beyond nearby purpose and desire eventually results in the creation of wider and farther-reaching purposes and enables us to use a much wider and deeper range of conditions and means than were expressed in the observation of primitive practical purposes. For the time being, however, the formation of theories demands a resolute turning aside from the needs of practical operations previously performed.

This detachment is peculiarly hard to secure in the case of those persons who are concerned with building up the scientific content of educational practices and arts. There is a pressure for immediate results, for demonstration of a quick, short-time span of usefulness in school. There is a tendency to convert the results of statistical inquiries and laboratory experiments into directions and rules for the conduct of school administration and instruction. Results tend to be directly grabbed, as it were, and put into operation by teachers. Then there is not the leisure for that slow and gradual independent growth of theories that is a necessary condition of the formation of a true science. This danger is peculiarly imminent in a science of education because its very recentness and novelty arouse skepticism as to its possibility and its value. The human desire to prove that the scientific mode of attack is really of value brings pressure to convert scientific conclusions into rules and standards of schoolroom practice.

It would perhaps be invidious to select examples too near to current situations. Some illustration, however, is needed to give definiteness to what has been said. I select an instance which is remote in time and crude in itself. An investigator found that girls between the ages of eleven and fourteen mature more rapidly than boys of the same age. From this fact, or presumed fact, he drew the inference that during these years boys and girls should be separated for purposes of instruction. He converted an intellectual finding into an immediate rule of school practice.

18

That the conversion was rash, few would deny. The reason is obvious. School administration and instruction is a much more complex operation than was the one factor contained in the scientific result. The significance of one factor for educational practice can be determined only as it is balanced with many other factors. Taken by itself, this illustration is so crude that to generalize from it might seem to furnish only a caricature. But the principle involved is of universal application. No conclusion of scientific research can be converted into an immediate rule of educational art. For there is no educational practice whatever which is not highly complex; that is to say, which does not contain many other conditions and factors than are included in the scientific finding.

Nevertheless, scientific findings are of practical utility, and the situation is wrongly interpreted when it is used to disparage the value of science in the art of education. What it militates against is the transformation of scientific findings into *rules* of action. Suppose for the moment that the finding about the different rates of maturing in boys and girls of a certain age is confirmed by continued investigation, and is to be accepted as fact. While it does not translate into a specific rule of fixed procedure, it is of some worth. The teacher who really knows this fact will have his personal attitude changed. He will be on the alert to make certain observations which would otherwise escape him; he will be enabled to interpret some facts which would otherwise be confused and misunderstood. This knowledge and understanding render his practice more intelligent, more flexible and better adapted to deal effectively with concrete phenomena of practice.

Nor does this tell the whole story. Continued investigation reveals other relevant facts. Each investigation and conclusion is special, but the tendency of an increasing number and variety of specialized results is to create new points of view and a wider field of observation. Various special findings have a cumulative effect; they reënforce and extend one another, and in time lead to the detection of principles that bind together a number of facts that are diverse and even isolated in their *prima facie* occurrence. These connecting principles which link different phenomena together we call laws.

Facts which are so interrelated form a system, a science. The practitioner who knows the system and its laws is evidently in possession of a powerful instrument for observing and interpreting what goes on before him. This intellectual tool affects his attitudes and modes of response in what he does. Because the range of understanding is deepened and widened he can take into account remote consequences which were originally hidden from view and hence were ignored in his actions. Greater continuity is introduced; he does not isolate situations and deal with them in separation as he was compelled to do when ignorant of connecting principles. At the same time, his practical dealings become more flexible. Seeing more relations he sees more possibilities, more opportunities. He is emancipated from the need of following tradition and special precedents. His ability to judge being enriched, he has a wider range of alternatives to select from in dealing with individual situations.

What Science Means

If we gather up these conclusions in a summary we reach the following results. In the first place, no genuine science is formed by isolated conclusions, no matter how scientifically correct the technique by which these isolated results are reached, and no matter how exact they are. Science does not emerge until these various findings are linked up together to form a relatively coherent system—that is, until they reciprocally confirm and illuminate one another, or until each gives the others added meaning. Now this development requires time, and it requiries more time in the degree in which the transition from an empirical condition to a scientific one is recent and hence imperfect.

Illustrations from the Physical Sciences

The physical sciences have a much longer past behind them than psychological and social inquiries. In addition, they deal with subjects that are intrinsically less complex, involving fewer variables. This difference in the degree of maturity is at the bottom of what was said regarding the danger of premature transfer of special scientific findings into educational practice. It explains why scientific investigations regarding educational problems must go on, for a considerable time, in comparative remoteness and detachment from direct application, and why the pressure to demonstrate *immediate* utility in school administration and instruction is dangerous.

The way in which physical science was put upon its present foundations proves the scientific necessity of knowledge of relationships forming a system; it proves also the dependence of this knowledge upon a scheme of *general thought*, if experiments and measurements are to have scientific value. The history of physics proves conclusively that measurements and correlations, no matter how quantitatively exact, cannot yield a science except in connection with general principles which indicate *what* measurement to conduct and *how* they are to be interperted. Galileo's experiments and measurements form the basis of modern science; they were made in connection with rolling of balls on an inclined plane, movements of pendulums and the dropping of balls from the Leaning Tower of Pisa.

Galileo had, however, first performed an experiment in thought, leading him to the hypothesis that the time of falling bodies is proportional to the square of the space traversed. It was this general idea, arrived at by thinking, that gave point to his experiment in Pisa, and that gave meaning to his measurement of the elapsed time of falling of bodies of various textures and volumes. His conception of what was measured, namely a generalization about relations of space, time and motion as the true objects of physical measurement, gave his measurements scientific status. Without these ideas he would not have known what to measure; he would have measured at random. Nor would he have known the meaning of his measurements after they were made; they would have remained mere intellectual curiosities.

It was also his preliminary hypotheses framed by thought which gave revolutionary import to his measurements of rolling balls. His experiments here and with pendulums went to confirm his theory that bodies in motion continue to move with the same velocity and direction unless externally acted upon. The result in connection with that at Pisa enabled acceleration to be measured and a general formula to be framed. In consequence, there was opened to subsequent experimenters the road of indirect measurement. Indirect measurements through calculation are much more important in science than are direct measurements, the latter merely supplying data and checks. The experimenters knew at the same time *what* they were measuring, namely, relations of mass, space, time, and motion. These general conceptions bound together their specific observations into a system.

[II]

BORROWED TECHNIQUES INSUFFICIENT

THESE considerations bring us to our second point, which is the negative side of our first. Educational science cannot be constructed simply by borrowing the techniques of experiment and measurement found in physical science. This could happen only if some way had been found by which mental or psychological phenomena are capable of statement in terms of units of space, time, motion, and mass. It is unnecessary to state that this condition has not been fulfilled. Nor have we as yet any *other* general hypotheses in the light of which to know *what* we are measuring and by which we can interpret results, place them in a system and lead on to fruitful indirect measurements. This principle is practically important at the present time. There is a tendency to assume that we are getting the material of a science of education merely because the techniques of older, better established sciences are borrowed and used.

It is no reproach to a would-be science that in early stages it makes experiments and measurements the results of which lack generalized significance. A period of groping is inevitable. But the lack of an intellectually coherent and inclusive system is a positive warning against attributing scientific value to results merely because they are reached by means of recognized techniques borrowed from sciences already established and are capable of being stated in quantitative formulæ. Quantity is not even the fundamental idea of mathematics.

LAWS VS. RULES

THE third point is that laws and facts, even
when they are arrived at in genuinely
scientific shape, do not yield *rules of practice.*
Their value for educational practice—and *all*
education is a mode of practice, intelligent or
accidental and routine—is indirect; it consists
in provision of *intellectual instrumentalities* to
be used by the educator. The meaning of this
statement, in the contrast it draws between rules
and intellectual instrumentalities, may be sug-
gested by an illustrative instance told me by a
friend. A manufacturer of paints utilizes results gained in the chemical laboratory. But
the results in the factory vary from those obtained in the laboratory by from twenty to two
hundred per cent. The first reaction might
seem to be that the scientifically obtained conclusions are of no practical use, at least in the
case of the larger divergence.

But the manufacturer does not draw this inference. What he is interested in is *improvement* of his factory practices, so that its operations give an increased yield in relation to the amount of labor and materials consumed. He is aware that factory conditions involve more variables, and variables harder to control, than are found in the conditions of laboratory experiment. The divergence of actual results from strictly scientific results is, therefore, a direction to him to observe more exactly and, upon a larger scale, all the conditions which affect his result. He notes variations in the time and temperature of different processes, the effect of surrounding heat and moistures, the reaction of gases incidentally generated, and so on. As he discovers that and how they affect his results he modifies his practical procedures. Thus he hopes to better his practice, each step calling attention to the influence of subtler and more obscure conditions which affect results, so that improvement is reasonably progressive.

If, in such a case, the manufacturer took the scientific data as a fixed rule, he would either follow it inflexibly with no improvement in the elimination of waste and loss; or, more likely, he would become disgusted with the discrepancies between laboratory and factory output, and would decide that science was not good for his purpose and fall back upon empirical procedures. Actually, he employs the scientific results as intellectual tools *in* his empirical procedures. That is, they *direct his attention,* in both observation and reflection, to conditions and relationships which would otherwise escape him. If we retain the word "rule" at all, we must say that scientific results furnish a rule for the conduct of *observations and inquiries,* not a rule for overt action. They function not directly with respect to practice and its results, but indirectly, through the medium of an altered mental attitude. The manufacturer becomes more efficient practically because he is more intelligent and complete in his observations, knowing what to look for, and is guided in his interpretation of what he sees because he now sees it in the light of a larger set of relationships.

Scientifically Developed Attitudes

If we turn from the scientific investigator to the administrator and teacher in the school and ask what is the bearing of these considerations upon the use to be practically made of scientific findings, the answer to be given is fairly clear. I knew a teacher in a training school for teachers who used to tell his students, "If you find that what I am telling you, or what another teacher here tells you, gets in the way of your common sense, of your use of your own judgment in an actual school situation, forget what you have learned and rely upon what your own judgment tells you is the best thing to do under the circumstances."

I never understood this saying to mean that the teacher thought that personal common-sense judgments and intuitions were the sole and sufficient guides of the teacher, or that he regarded the principles and facts which were taught to those in training of no practical value. I imagine that what he said was a negative way of stating that the value of the science, the history and philosophy of education acquired in the training school, resides in the enlightenment and guidance it supplies to observation and judgment of actual situations as they arise. If, in any particular case, the students saw no connection between what they had learned and the school situation, instead of trying to derive a rule from what they had learned they should depend upon their judgment as that had been developed by theoretical learnings and as these might operate unconsciously. In short, it was a way of saying that the value of definite instruction with respect to educational matters consists

31

in its effect upon the formation of personal attitudes of observing and judging.

SOURCES VS. CONTENT

THE net conclusion of our discussion is that the final reality of educational science is not found in books, nor in experimental laboratories, nor in the class-rooms where it is taught, but in the minds of those engaged in directing educational activities. Results may be scientific, short of their operative presence in the attitudes and habits of observation, judgment and planning of those engaged in the educative act. But they are not *educational* science short of this point. They are psychology, sociology, statistics, or whatever.

This is the point upon which my whole discussion turns. We must distinguish between the *sources of educational science* and scientific content. We are in constant danger of confusing the two; we tend to suppose that certain results, because they are scientific, are already educational science. Enlightenment, clarity and progress can come about only as we remember that such results are *sources* to be used, through the medium of the minds of educators, to make educational functions more intelligent.

Educative Processes as a Source

The first question which comes before us is what is the place and rôle of educative processes and results in the school, family, etc., when they are viewed as a *source?* The answer is (1) that educational *practices* provide the data, the subject-matter, which form the *problems* of inquiry. They are the sole source of the ultimate problems to be investigated. These educational practices are also (2) the final *test of value* of the conclusion of all researches. To suppose that scientific findings decide the value of educational undertakings is to reverse the real case. Actual activities in *educating* test the worth of the results of scientific results. They may be scientific in some other field, but not in education until they serve educational purposes, and whether they really serve or not can be found out only in practice. The latter comes first and last; it is the beginning and the close: the beginning, because it sets the problems which alone give to investigations educational point and quality; the close, because practice alone can test, verify, modify and develop the conclusions of these investigations. The position of scientific conclusions is intermediate and auxiliary.

Illustration from Engineering

The development of engineering science affords a pertinent illustration and confirmation. Men built bridges before there was any science of mathematics and physics. But with the latter development, with formulæ of mechanics, statics, thrusts, stresses and strains, there arose the possibility of building bridges more efficiently, and ability to build them under conditions which previous methods were incompetent to cope with. *Bridge building* sets problems to be dealt with theoretically. Mathematics and mechanics are the sciences which handle the question. But their results are tried out, confirmed or the contrary, in new practical enterprises of bridge building, and thus new material is acquired which sets new problems to those who use mathematics and physics as tools, and so on indefinitely.

There is a science of bridge building in the

sense that there is a certain body of *independent* scientific material, say mathematics and mechanics, from which selections may be made and the selections organized to bring about more effective solution in practice of the difficulties and obstructions that present themselves in actual building of bridges. It is the way the material is handled and organized with reference to a purpose that gives us a right to speak of a science of bridge building, although the building itself is an art, not a science. The sciences of mechanics and mathematics are, in themselves, the sciences which they are, not sciences of bridge building. They *become* the latter when selected portions of them are focused upon the problems presented in the art of bridge building.

SCIENCE OF EDUCATION NOT INDEPENDENT

Two conclusions as to the sources of educational science are now before us.

First, educational practices furnish the material that sets the problems of such a science, while sciences already developed to a fair state of maturity are the sources from which material is derived to deal intellectually with these problems. There is no more a special

35

independent science of education than there is of bridge making. But material drawn from *other* sciences furnishes the content of educational science when it is focused on the problems that arise in education.

Illustrations from Measurements

Illustrations may be given of the use of measurements to guide the intelligence of teachers instead of as dictating rules of action. Thus it is reported that teachers in a high school were puzzled by discrepancies between achievements and intelligence quotients. So one of the teachers was relieved of some of her classes to visit parents and homes and interview students. Within two years this had become a full time position, contacts with clinics and other public agencies established, and there was an extension of the concept "problem student" to include other types of maladjustment than the intellectual. Again it is reported that psychological ratings were used as tentative guides to shift children about till the place was found where they could do their best work. In other schools that have taken over more or less of the work of the juvenile court, truant officers, medical inspectors and visiting nurses, the I. Q. reports are correlated with factors ascertained in these other lines before there is direct use of them.* A homogeneous grouping without intervening inquiries approximates dangerously to transforming a theoretical finding into a rule of action.

It is empirically noted that one teacher has upon pupils an effect that is qualitatively termed inspiring, awakening, and that the personality of another teacher is relatively deadening, dulling. Now here is a problem set for inquiry, whether the sciences which have to be drawn upon are sufficiently advanced to provide material for its solution or not. In this case, the science upon which a draft must be made is presumably that of social psychology, dealing with the interactions of persons. The original facts are raw material, crude data. They are not part of the science save as they set the problem and give direction to inquiry: in so doing they may lead to developments within social psychology itself. But it is the latter which is the direct source of the content of educational science in this case.

If it is empirically noticed that the stimulat-

* The illustrations are taken from Thomas, W., and D. W. "The Child in America."

ing effect of some teachers is followed later on by a blasé indifference, or in emotional over-excitability, on the part of some students, a further problem is set, new discriminations have to be made, and so on.

It is noted that children in some rooms, or at certain times of day are languid and dull and work inefficiently. This condition, even on an empirical basis, raises the question of ventilation, heating, etc. There is a problem set for scientific inquiry. Not education but physiology and chemistry are the sources drawn upon. Some statement of the detailed correlation between conditions of air, temperature and moisture and the state of organic efficiency of pupils may be reached; a solution in terms of a definite mechanism, of *how* things are linked together.

Difficulties arising in temperament and deep-seated habits may be so great that the scientific result in the first case will not seriously affect the teacher whose influence on pupils is undesirable. But it *may* be of aid in correction of attitudes; and, in any case, it gives useful information to administrators in dealing with such persons. In the other instance, teachers have an intellectual ground for alertness in observing physical conditions in their classrooms and organic symptoms in their children that they did not have before. There is then a case of educational science in operation. What is done consists of acts, not of science. But science takes effect in rendering these activities more intelligent. If teachers are sufficiently alert and intelligent, they go on to notice conditions of the same general nature, but more subtle, and set a problem for further more refined inquiry. In any case, there will be a distinct difference in attitude between the teacher who merely puts into effect certain rules about opening windows, reducing temperature, etc., and the one who performed similar acts because of personal observation and understanding.

The Scientific Sources of Education

A further conclusion follows regarding the sciences that are the source of effective means for dealing with them. We may fairly enough call educational practice a kind of social engineering. Giving it that name at once provokes notice that as an art it is much more backward than branches of physical engineering, like land surveying, bridge-building and construction of railways. The reason is obvious. After all allowance is made for less systematic training for persons who engage in the art of education, the outstanding fact is that the sciences which must be drawn upon to supply scientific content to the work of the practitioner in education are themselves less mature than those which furnish the intellectual content of engineering. The human sciences that are sources of the scientific content of education—biology, psychology and sociology—for example, are relatively backward compared with mathematics and mechanics.

This statement is not an innocuous truism, for important consequences flow from taking it to heart. In the first place, just as the problems arising on the practical side in modern industry, for example, have been an important factor in stimulating researches in heat, electricity and light, so the problems that show themselves in educational practice should furnish agencies to direct the humane sciences into intellectually fruitful channels. It is not practice alone that has suffered from isolation of thinkers in the social and psychological disciplines from the occurrences taking place in schools. Indifference to the latter, a hardly veiled intellectual contempt for them, has undoubtedly strengthened the rule of convention, routine and accidental opinion in the schools. But it has also deprived the sciences in question of problems that would have stimulated significant inquiry and reflection. Much of the barrenness and loose speculation in the humane sciences is directly due to remoteness from the material that would stimulate, direct and test thought. Nothing in our recent situation is more promising for scientific development than the fact that the intellectual distance between university and elementary school, for example, is lessening.

In the second place, frank recognition of the relative backwardness of the sciences that must form the main content of educational science is a protection as well as a stimulus. Recognition that genuine growth in educational science is dependent upon prior advance in other subjects prevents us from entertaining premature and exaggerated expectations. It would, if fully recognized, deter workers in the field from efforts at premature introduction into school practice of materials whose real value lies only in the contribution they may make to the further building up of scientific content; it would militate against exploitation of results that are as yet only half-baked. And it would impress upon workers in the field of educational science the need for thorough equipment in the sciences upon which the science of education must draw.

At this point, the fact that educational practices are a source of the *problems* of educational science rather than of its definite material is especially significant. Adequate recognition that the source of the really scientific content is found in other sciences would compel attempt at mastery of what they have to offer. With respect to statistical theory this lesson has been pretty well learned. Whether it has been with respect to other disciplines, or even with respect to the separate and exclusive application of statistics to the solution of educational problems, is open to doubt.

Finally, recognition of this obvious fact would be a protection against attempting to extract from psychology and sociology definite solutions which it is beyond their present power to give. Such attempts, even when made unconsciously and with laudable intent to render education more scientific, defeat their own purpose and create reactions against the very concept of educational science. Learning to wait is one of the important things that scientific method teaches, and the extent in which this lesson has been learned is one fair measure of the claim to a hearing on the part of workers in the field of education.

THERE is a second and more positive connection between educational practices which set problems and the sciences that are sources of material for dealing with them. The objection to arm-chair science is not that thinking is done in arm-chairs. A certain amount of downright thinking going on quietly in the head is as necessary to the development of any science as is the activity of the senses and the hands in the laboratory. The arm-chair may be a good place in which to do this thinking. The objection is to the remoteness of the thinking which is done from the original source of intellectual supplies. This remoteness may exist in work done in laboratories as well as in the arm-chair of the study. It is found whenever there is lack of vital connection between the field-work practice and the research work.

The practical obstacles here are numerous. The research persons connected with school systems may be too close to the practical problems and the university professor too far away from them, to secure the best results. The former may get too entangled in immediate detailed problems for the best work. Minor problems for immediate solution may be put up to him and not leave him time for investigations

43

having a longer time-span. The latter may not have enough first-hand contact to discriminate the important problems from the secondary and the conditions which render them problems. He is then likely, also, to occupy himself with isolated and relatively trivial problems, a kind of scientific "busy-work," and yet may expect his results to be taken seriously by workers in the field.

Physical contact in any case is not so important as intellectual contact of a sympathetic sort. The indispensable necessity is that there be some kind of vital current flowing between the field worker and the research worker. Without this flow, the latter is not able to judge the real scope of the problem to which he addresses himself. He will not know enough of the conditions under which the particular problem presents itself in school to control his inquiry, nor be able to judge whether the resources of other sciences at his command enable him to deal with it effectively. Nor will he understand enough of the concrete situations under which his finally preferred solution is to be applied to know whether it is a real or an artificial and arbitrary solution. If it is the latter, it may succeed in dealing with the more obvious difficulties of a situation, the external symptoms, but fail to hit basic causes, and may even set up more difficult because more obscure and subtle complications when it is applied.

Illustrations from School Reports

The problem here is not, however, a one-sided one. It concerns the teacher and administrator, the field worker, as well as the researcher. Special conditions are required if the material of school practices is to be presented to others in such shape as to form the data of a problem. It perhaps suffices to refer, in illustration of this point, to the great improvement already brought in the handling of school reports, both administrative and instructional. Since the value of any piece of research is definitely conditioned by the data at command, it is almost impossible to put too much emphasis upon the importance of records and reports, and of the manner in which they are kept, qualitative as well as quantitative.

The value of this material to the investigator in education is almost like that of systematic and cumulative clinical records for medical science. There is an evident circle in this matter. The kind of reports that are asked for and secured depend upon the existing state of the science, upon the scientific interests that dominate at a particular time. They also furnish data for further inquiries and conclusions. Hence the need that they should not be too rapidly mechanized into a standard fixed form. There must be flexible room for change or else scientific arrest will come from a too rigid fixation of the molds in which data are cast.

The Teacher as Investigator

This factor of reports and records does not exhaust, by any means, the rôle of practitioners in building up a scientific content in educational activity. A constant flow of less formal reports on special school affairs and results is needed. Of the various possibilities here I select one for discussion. It seems to me that the contributions that might come from *class-room* teachers are a comparatively neglected field; or, to change the metaphor, an almost unworked mine. It is unnecessary to point out the large extent to which superintendents and principals have been drawn into the work of studying special problems and contributing material relative to them. It is to be hoped that the move-

46

ment will not cease until all active class-room teachers, of whatever grade, are also drawn in. There are undoubted obstacles in the way. It is often assumed, in effect if not in words, that class-room teachers have not themselves the training which will enable them to give effective intelligent coöperation. The objection proves too much, so much so that it is almost fatal to the idea of a workable scientific content in education. For these teachers are the ones in direct contact with pupils and hence the ones through whom the results of scientific findings finally reach students. They are the channels through which the consequences of educational theory come into the lives of those at school. I suspect that if these teachers are mainly channels of reception and transmission, the conclusions of science will be badly deflected and distorted before they get into the minds of pupils. I am inclined to believe that this state of affairs is a chief cause for the tendency, earlier alluded to, to convert scientific findings into recipes to be followed. The human desire to be an "authority" and to control the activities of others does not, alas, disappear when a man becomes a scientist.

A statistical study of, say the reports of the N. E. A., would show the actual percentage of contributions to educational discussion made by class-room teachers on that level. It would perhaps raise the query whether some of the incapacity, real or alleged, of this part of the corps of educators, the large mass of teachers, is not attributable to lack of opportunity and stimulus, rather than to inherent disqualifications. As far as schools are concerned, it is certain that the problems which require scientific treatment arise in actual relationships with students. Consequently, it is impossible to see how there can be an adequate flow of subject-matter to set and control the problems investigators deal with, unless there is active particiation on the part of those directly engaged in teaching.

NO INTRINSIC EDUCATIONAL SCIENCE CONTENT

If we now turn to the subjects from which are drawn the materials that are to be brought to bear upon educational problems, we are forced to recognize a fact already incidentally noted. There is no subject-matter intrinsically marked off, earmarked so to say, as the content of educational science. Any methods and any facts and principles from any subject whatsoever that enable the problems of administration and instruction to be dealt with in a bettered way are pertinent. Thus, in all that concerns the bearing of physical conditions upon the success of school work—as in the case of ventilation, temperature, etc., already mentioned—physiology and related sciences are sources of scientific content. In other problems, such as making budgets, cost-accountings, etc., economic theory is drawn upon. It may be doubted whether with reference to some aspect or other of education there is any organized body of knowledge that may not need to be drawn upon to become a source of educational science.

This consideration explains many phenomena in the present situation. It accounts for the rapid growth of interest in the development of scientific content for educational practices in so many different lines of activity. We have become only recently alive to the complexity of the educative process and aware of the number and variety of disciplines that must contribute if the process is to go on in an intelligently directed way. In accounting for the manifestation of enthusiastic activity on the part of some, the situation also explains the skeptical indifference of many about the whole matter. Not merely inert conservatives in the general public but many professors in other lines in universities have not been awakened to the complexity of the educational undertaking. Hence, such persons regard the activities of those in departments of education as futile and void of serious meaning.

Failure to perceive that educational science has no content of its own leads, on the other hand, to a segregation of research which tends to render it futile. The assumption, if only tacit, that educational science has its own peculiar subject-matter results in an isolation which makes the latter a "mystery" in the sense in which the higher crafts were once mysteries. A superficial token of this isolation is found in the development of that peculiar terminology that has been called "pedageese." Segregation also accounts for the tendency, already mentioned, to go at educational affairs without a sufficient grounding in the non-educational disciplines that must be drawn upon, and hence to exaggerate minor points in an absurdly one-sided way, and to grasp at some special scientific technique as if its use were a magical guarantee of a scientific product.

Recognition of the variety of sciences that must be focused when solving any educational problem tends to breadth of view and to more serious and prolonged effort at balance of the variety of factors which enter into even the simplest problems of teaching and administration. The uncontrolled succession of waves of one-sided temporarily dominating interests and slogans that have affected educational practice and theory could thus be reduced.

SPECIAL SOURCES

IN spite of the wide and indeterminate field of sciences that are sources of scientific content in education, there are certain subjects that occupy a privileged position. By common consent, I suppose, psychology and sociology hold such positions. The philosophy of education is a source of the science of education, but one less often recognized as such. We are, I think, habituated to thinking of the sciences as feeders of philosophy rather than of philosophy as a source of science. Philosophy is looked at by those who dignify it as a subject which analyzes critically the premises that are uncritically assumed in the special sciences, or else as a complete intellectual organization of their results. Others take a less respectful and perhaps more popular view of it, and regard it as a constantly vanishing quantity, dealing by way of opinion and speculation with matters that sciences have not got around to dealing with in a positive way. Personally, I think there is truth in both of these views, but that neither one touches the heart of the relationship of philosophy and science. There is in every subject at every time a serial progression from the more specific to the more general. The only distinction we can profitably draw is to say that science lies toward the specific pole and philosophy toward the general, while there is no definite line where one leaves off and the other begins.

It is because of this fact that there is a reciprocal relation between them, each feeding the other as a source. Were this the time and place, it could be shown from the history of the sciences, mathematical, physical and biological, that ideas originating at the philosophic end (general, often vague and speculative, if you please) have been indispensable factors in the generation of science. An examination of history would also show that there is no steady one-way movement; the movement from general to special is not one that has a definite conclusion that stays put. Specialized results recurrently get too set and rigid because of isolation due to the very specialization by which they are obtained. Fermentation and fructification then come in from the pole of general ideas and points of view. Specific results are shaken up, loosened and placed in new contexts.

Illustrations

The revolution in astronomical and physical science effected by Galileo, Descartes and Newton is a case in point. The controlling hypotheses were derived from philosophic ideas that seemed to their early contemporaries highly speculative. The idea of "evolution" was developed in philosophy before it made its appearance in biology. Metaphysical speculations regarding the relation of mind and body conditioned the creation and growth of physiological psychology.

These illustrations do not prove that the influence of philosophy as a source of science has been wholly to the good. On the contrary, there have been in every instance hang-overs from earlier philosophies which have been detrimental, and which have had to be eliminated from science with toil and pain. But aside from the fact that new general ideas have always played a part in finally getting rid of these hang-overs, it is an undeniable fact that the human mind works in this way, and that whether desirable or undesirable, it cannot be eliminated.

Hypotheses

If we ask why this should be so, we are at once confronted with the rôle of *hypotheses* in every scientific undertaking, because of the necessary place they occupy in every intellectual operation. Hypotheses form a scale from more general to more specific, and at every point the more general ones affect the more specific. This fact of dependence is overlooked only because the more general one is so incorporated in the special and detailed ones that it is forgotten. Then some crisis in scientific development leads to its detection and revision. Physical science is at present undergoing precisely such a reconstruction.

Philosophy of education is, accordingly, a source of the science of education in the degree in which it provides working hypotheses of comprehensive application. Both "working" and "hypotheses" are important. It is hypotheses, not fixed and final principles or truths that are provided; they have to be tested and modified as they are used in suggesting and directing the detailed work of observation and understanding. They are *working* ideas; special investigations become barren and one-sided in the degree in which they are conducted without reference to a wider, more general view. This statement is particularly applicable in the early stages of formation of a new science. Physics, chemistry, biology, all have behind them a history that has put them in possession of relatively tested and solid general principles. Just because educational science has no such achievement of laws to fall back upon, it is in a tentative and inchoate state which renders it especially in need of direction by large and fruitful hypotheses. No matter how these are obtained, they are intrinsically philosophical in nature, good or bad philosophy as the case may be. To treat them as scientific rather than as philosophic is to conceal from view their hypothetical character and to freeze them into rigid dogmas that hamper instead of assisting actual inquiry.

The Purpose of the Philosophy of Education

It is sometimes said that philosophy is concerned with determining the ends of education while the science of education determines the means to be used. As one who is a philosopher

55

rather than a scientist I might be inclined to welcome a statement that confers upon philosophy such an honorable position. Without a good deal of interpretation, it is, however, likely to give rise to more false than true conceptions. In this interpretation there are two important considerations.

In the first place, the notion easily gives rise to, even if it does not logically imply, a misapprehension of the relation of a philosophy of education to educational practices and direct experience in the field. In any vital sense it is these practices which determine educational ends. Concrete educational experience is the primary source of all inquiry and reflection because it sets the problems, and tests, modifies, confirms or refutes the conclusions of intellectual investigation. The philosophy of education neither originates nor settles ends. It occupies an intermediate and instrumental or regulative place. Ends actually reached, consequences that actually accrue, are surveyed, and their values estimated in the light of a general scheme of values.

But if a philosophy starts to reason out its conclusions without definite and constant regard to the concrete experiences that define the problem for thought, it becomes speculative in a way that justifies contempt. As far as ends

56

and values are concerned, the empirical material that is necessary to keep philosophy from being fantastic in content and dogmatic in form is supplied by the ends and values which are produced in educational processes as these are actually executed. What a philosophy of education can contribute is range, freedom and constructive or creative invention. The worker in any field gets preoccupied with more immediate urgencies and results. When one begins to extend the range, the scope, of thought, to consider obscure collateral consequences that show themselves in a more extensive time-span, or in reference to an enduring development, that one begins to philosophize whether the process is given that name or not. What is *termed* philosophy is only a more systematic and persistent performance of this office.

What I have termed the contribution of "freedom," of liberation, is a necessary accompaniment of this breadth of survey of actual ends or consequences. The professional practitioner in any field, from a factory to a church and schoolhouse, is in danger of getting tied down, of getting habit-bound, compensating for this rigidity by impulsive excursions, undertaken according to temperament and circumstance, when routine becomes intolerable. I do not say that philosophers see life steadily and

57

see it whole; complete achievement in this respect is humanly impossible. But *any one* is philosophical in the degree in which he makes a consistent effort in this direction. The result is emancipation. When this liberation is confined with the mind, the inner consciousness, of any one, it affords intense personal gratification, but it effects nothing and becomes specious. Its effect is found only in operation. For a philosophy of education this operation is found in enabling practitioners to carry on their work in a more liberal spirit, with escape from tradition and routine and one-sided personal interests and whims.

This contribution is made by way of the third function mentioned; namely, constructive imagination and invention. It is not enough to criticize the narrow limitations of accepted ends and values. This needful task is but the negative side of the function of suggesting new ends, new methods, new materials. In performing this office, provision of scope of estimate and liberation of mind comes to a head. As far as the philosophy of education effects anything important, this is what it accomplishes for those who study it. Ideas are ideas, that is, suggestions for activities to be undertaken, for experiments to be tried. The proof of the pudding is in the eating. The philosophy of education not only draws its original material as to ends and value from actual experience in education, but it goes back to these experiences for testing, confirmation, modification, and the provision of further materials. This is what is meant when it is said that its work is intermediate and instrumental, not original nor final.

Our other point concerns the relations of science and philosophy with respect to means and ends. The statement as often made gives rise to misapprehension. It leads to the notion that means and ends are separate from each other, each having its own fixed province. In reality, ends that are incapable of realization are ends only in name. Ends must be framed in the light of available means. It may even be asserted that ends are only means brought to full interaction and integration. The other side of this truth is that means are fractional parts of ends. When means and ends are viewed as if they were separate, and to be dealt with by different persons who are concerned with independent provinces, there is imminent danger of two bad results.

Ends, values, become empty, verbal; too remote and isolated to have more than an emotional content. Means are taken to signify means already at hand, means accepted because they are already in common use. As far as this view prevails, the work of a science of education is reduced to the task of refining and perfecting the existing mechanism of school operations. Lack of efficiency, unnecessary waste, in the teaching of reading, writing, numbers, history, geography are detected so that they may be eliminated. More efficient methods of accomplishing the ends that already obtain are devised. This is good as far as it goes. But it overlooks a fundamental issue. How far do the existing ends, the actual consequences of current practices go, even when perfected? The important problem is devising *new* means in contradistinction to improved use of means already given. For "new means" does not signify merely new ways of accomplishing more efficiently ends already current, but means that will yield consequences, ends, that are qualitatively different. We can assign means to science and ends to philosophy only under the condition that there be persistent and unremitting interaction between the two.

Psychology

Little space remains in which to consider psychology and sociology as sources of educational science. However, the considerations already adduced supply, I think, suggestions by which many of the most important issues in these fields may be dealt with. For example, there is general agreement that psychology lies nearer to the question of means and the social sciences nearer to that of ends, or that the first is more closely connected with *how* pupils learn, whether knowledge or skill, and the latter with *what* they are to learn. But such a statement only brings us to the threshold of the problem of the relation between the "how" and the "what," means and ends. If the how and the what, the psychological and the social, method and subject matter, must interact coöperatively in order to secure good results, a hard and fast distinction between them is fraught with danger. We want a method that will select subject-matter that aids psychological development, and we want a subject-matter that will secure the use of methods psychologically correct. We cannot begin by dividing the field between the psychology of individual activity and growth and studies or subject-matters that are socially desirable, and then expect that at the end in practical operation the two things will balance each other.

An unbiased survey of the situation will, I think, show that the danger is not merely theoretical. When we make a sharp distinction between *what* is learned and *how* we learn it, and assign the determination of the process of learning to psychology and of subject-matter to social science, the inevitable outcome is that the reaction of what is studied and learned upon the development of the person learning, upon the tastes, interests, and habits that control his future mental attitudes and responses is overlooked. In that degree the psychological account of the process of personal learning and growth is deficient and distorted. It then deals with a short segment of the learning process instead of with its continuities.

Social needs and conditions are said to dictate, for example, the necessity of instruction in reading, writing and number at a fairly early age. It is also recognized that these are useful factors in later personal growth, being the means of opening up learning in a variety of subjects. So far the two aspects seem to be in harmony. But suppose the question of how children learn most effectively to master these skills then be taken up in isolation, and methods are devised to promote the ready acquisition of the skills in question. The larger question is what other habits, including tastes and desires, are being collaterally formed.

That a person can learn efficiently to read

and yet not form a taste for reading good literature, or without having curiosities aroused that will lead him to apply his ability to read to explore fields outside of what is conventionally termed good reading matter, are sad facts of experience. Learning to read may develop book-worms, children who read omnivorously, but at the expense of development of social and executive abilities and skills. The question of *what* one learns to read is thus inextricably bound up with the question of *how* one learns to read. Unfortunately, experience shows that the methods which most readily and efficiently bring about skill to read (or write, or figure) in its narrower sense of ability to recognize, pronounce and put together words, do not at the same time take care of the formation of attitudes that decide the uses to which the ability is to be put. This is the more important issue.

It will not do for the psychologist to content himself with saying in effect: "These other things are none of my business; I have shown how the child may most readily and efficiently form the skill. The rest is up to somebody else." It will not do because one skill is acquired, other abilities, preferences and disabilities are also learned, and these fall within the province of the psychological inquirer. This conclusion does not mean that the demonstration of how a particular skill is most readily formed is of no value. But it does mean that educationally speaking the problems of attendant radiations, expansions and contractions, are in the end more important, and that it is dangerous to take the part for the whole. Nor is it satisfactory to say that the part must be mastered before the whole can be attacked. For, by the nature of the case, the whole enters into the part, that is, it is a determining factor in the *way* in which one learns to read. Thus the consideration of how one learns to read in its connection with its effect upon future personal development and interests demands attention to desirable subject-matter. The social question is intertwined with the psychological.

Qualitative vs. Quantitative Values

Interdependence determines the limits of quantitative measurements for educational science. That which can be measured is the specific, and that which is specific is that which can be isolated. The prestige of measurements in physical science should not be permitted to blind us to a fundamental educational issue: How far is education a matter of forming specific skills and acquiring special bodies of information which are capable of isolated treatment? It is no answer to say that a human being is always occupied in acquiring a special skill or a special body of facts, if he is learning anything at all. This is true. But the *educational* issue is what *other* things in the way of desires, tastes, aversions, abilities and disabilities he is learning along with his specific acquisitions.

The control of conditions demanded by laboratory work leads to a maximum of isolation of a few factors from other conditions. The scientific result is rigidly limited to what is established with these other conditions excluded. In educating individualities, no such exclusion can be had. The number of variables that enter in is enormous. The intelligence of the teacher is dependent upon the extent in which he takes into account the variables that are not obviously involved in his immediate special task. Judgment in such matter is of qualitative situations and must itself be qualitative.

The parent and educator deal with situations that never repeat one another. Exact quantitative determinations are far from meeting the demands of such situations, for they presuppose repetitions and exact uniformities. Exaggeration of their importance tends to cramp judgment, to substitute uniform rules for the free play of thought, and to emphasize the mechanical factors that also exist in schools. They contribute at most to the more efficient working of present practices in some subjects. They have already been fruitful in securing eliminations, especially in the more routine skills, such as the three R's. But they do not give any help in larger questions of reconstruction of curriculum and methods. What is worse, they divert attention and energy from the need of reconstructions due to change of social conditions and to the inertia of traditions of the school system.

More important psychological contributions may be expected from the psychology of individual growth. The greatest aid at this point is to be derived from biological psychology, social psychology and psychiatry. Biology is not at present in any large measure a quantitative science, and only harm can result from the attempt to build up a scientific content of education that skips over the biological sciences and allies itself with the physical and mathematical, those furthest remote from the needs, problems and activities of human beings. In the biological field, general considerations regarding processes of development are more fundamental than is the anatomy of the nervous system. The latter is important, but it is dangerous to build educational theory upon details selected from what is known and current at a particular time.

_____

Illustration from S-R Psychology

The stimulus-response psychology in the form in which it prevails at the present time, is an illustration. There is no doubt that the stimulus-response idea presents a truth of great value. But just now it tends to be interpreted in a way that isolates a particular narrow part of it, based on the mechanisms of reflex actions, from the general course of biological development. Then the idea of the bond that connects stimulus and response is taken to be of a hard and fast performed character, instead of a flexible and functional one. In addition, the place of any particular S-R bond in the entire system of behavior is overlooked, or else the whole system is reduced to an algebraic summation of original fixed, isolated units. The important activities of the sympathetic nervous system, and the fact that even the reflexes function in the service of needs of the whole system is overlooked. Moreover, particular S-R connections interpreted on the basis of isolated reflexes, are viewed as static cross-sections, and the factor most important in education, namely, the longitudinal, the temporal span of growth and change is neglected.

Illustration from Psychiatry

In many respects the findings of social psychology and psychiatry reënforce each other. For the latter has clearly brought out that most arrests of development, fixations and morbid human attitudes, are due to the reaction of association with others back upon the formation of attitudes and their subsequent career. The most harmful and undesirable emotional attitudes of children, so fundamental in development, especially fears, inferiorities, etc., have been shown to be due mainly to social conditioning. It has been practically demonstrated that no amount of repetition really fixes a habit apart from attendant emotional responses, and that these are influenced by association with others. Opportunities for constant success and positive achievement have been shown to be indispensable conditions for preventing the growth of inferiority complexes. The unconscious character of the major part of human motivation reveals the unwisdom of determining the selection of the activities of children on the basis of what they say when asked what they want to do—indeed of being very sparing in asking the question. It also forces greater attention to the attitudes that control, unconsciously, the dealings of adults with the young. Most positively of all, it compels constant attention to what children actually do in order that there may be ability to understand the forces that actually move them in their behavior.

No apology is made for emphasis upon the psychiatric side. The increasing number of insane and neurotics is itself evidence of great failure and evil in our educational processes, parental and scholastic. Even more significant is the discovery in psychiatry itself of the number of morbid displacements, injurious to both happiness and social usefulness, found in persons called normal. Conventional and traditional methods, in instruction and discipline, are continuously engaged in manufacturing morbid fixations and dislocations. But when the latter reveal themselves they are usually attributed to some inherent psychological cause, some element of defect or perversity, inherent in the human nature of those taught, while in fact by far the greater part of them are induced growths, having their cause in the relations set up in some social contact. A knowledge of social psychology in connection with psychiatry, both being used to interpret the processes of normal physiological activity, are indispensable to any rounded out scientific content for educational activity.

Sociology

I come now to the contribution of sociology —by which for present purposes I mean all the social disciplines—to the scientific content of education. Fortunately, it is not necessary to insist at this day and date upon the importance of this factor. Like the word "social," the words "socialized education" are in the air. The questions that call for discussion concern how the idea is to be interpreted. Time permits of mention of only two points. One relates to the position of *social tools*. The most obvious example of such tools is skill in language (reading, spelling and writing) and number. But these are only instances. Manners also form a social tool and so do morals in one of its aspects. A considerable portion of geography and history do so, and also elementary science, as well as some traits of the fine arts. In fact, it would be hard to draw a line at any point in the educational scheme; consider, for example, the necessities of the professional students in medicine and law to master certain skills and bodies of fact as social tools. The only difference among subjects of the curriculum as to social tools seems to be a matter of degree.

In view of this fact, the current habit of speaking only of some skills as social tools suggests the need for thought. The cause for their being selected as *the* social tools becomes evident, I think, when we notice that the things usually called social tools are the most *formal* parts of the curriculum. These subjects and skill in employing them are formal because they are separated from social content; they are social tools prospectively rather than at the time they are learned. Emphasis upon repetition, making their acquisition a frequency function, is proof of this isolation from direct social subject-matter and value.

I am not going to discuss this point. I use it as an illustration of the current division, found in many subjects, between social tools and social consequences. The net effect of this division upon the contribution social subject-matter makes to educational science is serious. The tools that are recognized to be social are not treated socially but are relegated to the mechanics of psychology. In so far as they are not socially controlled, the social use to which

they are finally put is accidental. School practices are in this respect, in many modern
schools, ahead of theory. Those engaged in
the act of teaching know that the social tools
are best acquired in a social context and for
the sake of some social application falling
within a nearby phase of life.

When skill in and with tools is not socially
formed, that is, generated for social ends, the
latter are separated from the means by which
they should be controlled. To take just one
instance: The kind of reading-matter that now
most abounds socially, as may be gathered
from a glance at newsstands, is largely of a
socially *undesirable* character. Yet it can be
sold only to readers, to those in possession of
the so-called social tools. Pages of exposition
would not speak more eloquently of what is
bound to happen when educational theory sepa-
rates, in the name of science, the psychological
processes that regulate the mere mechanism of
acquiring a skill from the social conditions and
needs which have to do with the application of
that skill.

The other point about the contribution of
sociology to educational science concerns the
determination of values, of objectives. The
shortest cut to get something that looks scientific is to make a statistical study of existing

72

practices and desires, with the supposition that their accurate determination will settle the subject-matter to be taught, thus taking curriculum-forming out of the air, putting it on a solid factual basis. This signifies, in effect and in logic, that the kind of education which the social environment gives unconsciously and in connection with all its defects, perversions and distortions, is the kind of education the schools should give consciously. Such an idea is almost enough to cause one to turn back to the theories of classicists who would confine the important subject-matter of instruction to the best of the products of the past, in disregard of present and prospective social conditions. It is hard to see any cause for such a procedure except a desire to demonstrate the value of "educational science" by showing that it has something immediate and direct to furnish in the guidance of schools.

EDUCATIONAL VALUES

This matter opens up the field of educational values and objectives. How are they to be determined? From what are they derived? The assumption that gives rise to the procedures just criticized is the belief that social conditions determine educational objectives. This is a fallacy. Education is autonomous and should be free to determine its own ends, its own objectives. To go outside the educational function and to borrow objectives from an external source is to surrender the educational cause. Until educators get the independence and courage to insist that educational aims are to be formed as well as executed within the educative process, they will not come to consciousness of their own function. Others will then have no great respect for educators because educators do not respect their own social place and work.

Such a statement will seem to many persons both absurd and presumptuous. It would be presumptuous if it had been said that *educators* should determine objectives. But the statement was that the *educative process* in its integrity and continuity should determine them. Educators have a place in this process, but they are not it, far from it. The notion that it is absurd springs from failure to view the function in its entirety. For education is itself a process of discovering what values are worth while and are to be pursued as objectives. To see what is going on and to observe the results of what goes on so as to see their further consequences in the process of growth, and so on indefinitely, is the only way in which the value of what takes place can be judged. To look to some outside source to provide aims is to fail to know what education is as an ongoing process. What a society is, it is, by and large, as a product of education, as far as its animating spirit and purpose are concerned. Hence it does not furnish a standard to which education is to conform. It supplies material by which to judge more clearly what education as it has been carried on has done to those who have been subjected to it. Another conclusion follows. There is no such thing as a fixed and final set of objectives, even for the time being or temporarily. Each day of teaching ought to enable a teacher to revise and better in some respect the objectives aimed at in previous work.

In saying these things, I am only recurring in another form to the idea with which I set out. The scientific content of education consists of whatever subject-matter, selected from other fields, enables the educator, whether administrator or teacher, to see and to think more clearly and deeply about whatever he is doing. Its value is not to supply objectives to him, any more than it is to supply him with ready-made rules. Education is a mode of life, of action. As an act it is wider than science. The latter, however, renders those who engage in the act more intelligent, more thoughtful, more aware of what they are about, and thus rectify and enrich in the future what they have been doing in the past. Knowledge of the objectives which society actually strives for and the consequences actually attained may be had in some measure through a study of the social sciences. This knowledge may render educators more circumspect, more critical, as to what they are doing. It may inspire better insight into what is going on here and now in the home or school; it may enable teachers and parents to look further ahead and judge on the basis of consequences in a longer course of developments. But it must operate through their own ideas, plannings, observations, judgments. Otherwise it is not *educational* science at all, but merely so much sociological information.

GENERAL CONCLUSION

THE sources of educational science are any portions of ascertained knowledge that enter into the heart, head and hands of educators, and which, by entering in, render the performance of the educational function more enlightened, more humane, more truly educational than it was before. But there is no way to discover what *is* "more truly educational" except by the continuation of the educational act itself. The discovery is never made; it is always making. It may conduce to immediate ease or momentary efficiency to seek an answer for questions outside of education, in some material which already has scientific prestige. But such a seeking is an abdication, a surrender. In the end, it only lessens the chances that education in actual operation will provide the materials for an improved science. It arrests growth; it prevents the thinking that is the final source of all progress. Education is by its nature an endless circle or spiral. It is an activity which *includes* science within itself. In its very process it sets more problems to be further studied, which then react into the educative process to change it still further, and thus demand more thought, more science, and so on, in everlasting sequence.